BEING, THERE

Being There

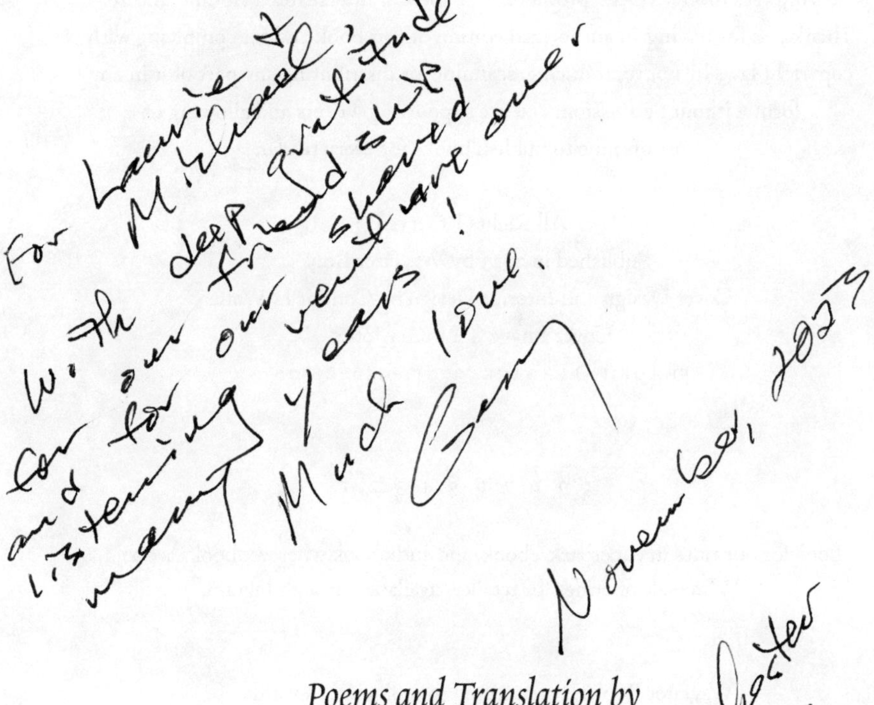

Poems and Translation by

Gary Whited

Published in 2023 by Wayfarer Books
Cover Design and Interior Design by Connor L. Wolfe
Cover Image © Hunter Jones
TRADE PAPERBACK 978-1-956368-77-2

10 9 8 7 6 5 4 3 2 1

Look for our titles in paperback, ebook, and audiobook wherever books are sold.
Wholesale offerings for retailers available through Ingram.

Wayfarer Books is committed to ecological stewardship.
We greatly value the natural environment and invest in conservation.
For each book purchased in our online store we plant one tree.

PO Box 1601, Northampton, MA 01060

860.574.5847 | info@homeboundpublications.com

HOMEBOUNDPUBLICATIONS.COM & WAYFARERBOOKS.ORG

Dedicated to my friend and poetry mentor,
David Ferry

and to the memory of my friend and philosophy mentor,
Henry Bugbee

The name for what, alone, is fully untroubled is *to be.*

PARMENIDES, FRAGMENT XX

TABLE OF CONTENTS

One

First Astonishments 3
How I Remember You 5
Walk This Creek Again 6
Locus Amoenus 7
The Fly and Me 9
One Fork Full at a Time 10
Horses Could Take You There 12

Two

Parmenides, Fragment I 15
Eléa's Gate 17
December 18
Touched by Stones 20

Three

Parmenides, Fragment II 25
Learning to Speak Fencepost 26
Right There 27
Parmenides, Fragment III 28
Winnowing 29
What Touched My Shoulder 30
Philosopher 31
Parmenides, Fragment IV 32
That Sound 33
The Way A Stone 35

Four

Parmenides, Fragment V 39
Any Day by Shadwell Creek 40
Parmenides, Fragment VI 42
Take 43
Cantilevered 44
Parmenides, Fragment VII 45
That Want in My Hand 46

Five

Parmenides, Fragment VIII 51
Bull Butte 55
Aurora Borealis 57

Six

Parmenides, Fragment IX 61
Ink and Sin 62
Parmenides, Fragment X 65
An Unexpected Quiet 66
Parmenides, Fragment XI 67
Heavenly Milk 68
Parmenides, Fragment XII 69
It Goes On 70
Deep Disturbance 72

Seven

Parmenides, Fragment XIII 75
Juneberry Picking 76
Parmenides, Fragment XIV 77
Him on His White Horse, Me on My Pinto 78
Spike 80
Parmenides, Fragment XV 82
It's Winter 83
Getting to Zero 85

Eight

Parmenides, Fragment XVI 89
Someplace 90
The Day I Stopped Hunting Deer 91
Parmenides, Fragment XVII 92
Remembering the First Time I See an Elephant 93
Two Infinities 95

Nine

Parmenides, Fragment XIX 99
Note to Parmenides 100
My Father's Visit 101
The Open and Close of It 103

Acknowledgments 107
Notes
About the Author
About the Press

ONE

First Astonishments

I cannot name what carries itself
In the curl of the pigs' tails trembling
As they arrive at the V-shaped feed trough

When I come near, bucket full of ground oats
Heavy against one leg, bucket of kitchen slop
Splashes at the other. Oats first, slop on top.

I listen close as their rubbery snouts plunge
And snort into the feast. Up high the soft,
Steady voice of wind sings above this slurping,

Presses its shoulder against the windmill's blades.
The giant wheel turns in circles. Each time
It goes 'round its metal to metal squeak

And grind carves the sky in half, pushes the wobbly,
Wooden stick down into the well beneath
The ground then lifts up water. Each time it

Descends the long stick bends so that I fear
It will break in two, but it doesn't. I watch
The clear water catch the light as it spills

From the end of the iron pipe into the wooden
Tank where stands our one Holstein who gives us milk.
In her slow cow way she quietly lowers her

Dark nose and curved mouth into the glistening
Water, drinks the cool liqueur into her boney
Body, silent but for the dim throaty sounds

Her gullet makes as she swallows. Her tail
Swishes side to side, pushes away flies
That feed on her rugged hide. I stand still

As a stone, look for where it all begins or ends.
My gaze travels from her tail to the pigs' tails,
Back and forth, gathers in the wind, the windmill,

The water and morning's shimmering light
Until the now silent Holstein's drunk her fill
And the pigs have slicked their trough.

HOW I REMEMBER YOU

Standing by a fencepost, puzzled,
Dazzled by its grains worn smooth

From the hairy hides of cows pressing
Against the post as they pass, red white-faced

Herefords, quiet when they walk but for the
Dry hoof-clack in summer, the high-pitched squeak

Of frozen snow under-hoof in winter.
Here you stand beside the corner post

More exposed than most, harvesting your
Delight in the surprise of smoothness, coming

From whatever rough edge has afflicted someone,
Maybe you, your cheek or your palm warmed

By the sun-warmed smooth place, your gaze fixed there,
As though your life depends on it.

Walk This Creek Again

My twig crack step on a small dried limb,
the deer down creek lifts her head,
cocks her ear my way, sniffs her air.

The next twig crack, she vaults up the bank
glides over the north pasture
owning something.

Makes me walk this creek again,
wanting once more to hear its silence break,
by me, then by her.

I walk, I watch,
sooner or later,
a twig,

a dried leaf maybe,
my footfall rustles loose
that small sound.

I stop, I listen for her escape,
see her bounding flight,
want that.

Locus Amoenus

...for true perception requires stillness
in the presence of things, the active, open reception
of the limitless gift of things.
—Henry Bugbee

I had no name for this delight that leapt from my eyes,
went out to meet things of the prairie I loved as a child.
Now I unroll each memory of these earthly things
that give themselves fully, not spent in their giving,
but some way added to;

glistening spittle from cows' mouths as they walk to water,
their afternoon grazing behind them, cuds chewed, swaying
along the same dusty path that always leads to water;

creek moving by twists and turns toward the Yellowstone river,
its coolness in summer, its shelter in winter, holding me
no matter how I come to it from the barn where
I spend hours lost in looking;

imprint of a hammer blow that missed the mark when men
were building this barn I gaze upon years beyond its making.
In haste one brought his hammer short of the mark,
clean look of this board forever changed;

above it near the rafters, spider-spun webbing,
each strand carrying years of dust since one day
when not just any spider, but that very one,

moved by what moves spiders, came upon this joint
of wood, made web to capture prey to live upon,
to spin again and again the weapon, fine and enough;

across the barnyard the corral gate sags on its hinges,
tilts the corner post from its standing straight,
sways in summer afternoon breezes when left
unlatched, and as it sways sends out
its ancient tone of longing...

The Fly and Me

The fly buzzing at the hayloft door
when I was a boy

and landing, silent, on the board
above the door,

is she still there if I remember her?
Or the one that landed

on the edge of the milk bucket
when I was learning to milk the cow,

and I watched her walk
all around the pail's edge

feeling intimate with this creature
as she made her way around the rim held tight

between my knees, the milk hissing
and foaming into itself, each of us in quest

of a next meal in this barn where the fly
would likely spend her entire life,

while I had not yet begun
to imagine mine.

One Fork Full at a Time

Cleaning the barn
lifted our spirits

like nothing else did.
Taking away the dung-filled straw

down to clean dirt
seemed to raise the barn's ceiling.

On rainy days,
no work in the field,

we grabbed our pitch-forks,
leaned into the heft and smell

of winter's give-off,
lifting it free

while rain fell
one drop at a time

and the manure pile grew
one fork full at a time

as the windmill turned
in a steady wind

lifting water
from the dark earth.

So many things
we could not know from here,

though what we knew
kept us faithful to our task,

waiting for the light
to return.

Horses Could Take You There

If I could remember it and the names of the horses
But I don't until stuck in traffic on the Jamaicaway

And the Red-Tail lands on a nearby limb
The horses' names start to come back

Goldie, Red, Lightning, Lucky, Blue, Babe and Spike
The young Sharp-Shinned I killed at the creek back then

Shooting BB's, again and again, the young hawk perfectly still
My body filled with sorrow, sound of my mother's accordion

The only thing that soothed—if I'd ever believed in a god,
This would be the time to unfold it—travel to the other world

Was possible according to Parmenides, horses could take you there
So quiet, the way Spike loped across the summer pasture

Two

Parmenides, Fragment I

Horses carry me as far as my longing can reach,
Transport me to the many-voiced road of the Goddess
That carries the one who listens through vast silence.
On that way I am carried, for the very wise horses
Know where to go. They pull the chariot at full gallop,
And maidens lead the way. An axle blazes
In its sockets—urged forward at both ends by its whirling
Wheels—sends forth the eerie sound of a whistle
You hear traveling to the other world. These young
Women, daughters of the sun, as they leave the house
Of night, throw back veils from their faces with their
Hands, and hasten to convey me into the light.
There stand the gates of the ways of Night and Day,
Enclosed with a lintel above and a stone threshold below.
These ethereal gates themselves are covered
With great doors whose alternating bolts are held fast
By Diké, Goddess of Justice, who lets nothing past her.
Speaking gentle words, the maidens cunningly
Persuade her to swiftly push back the bolted holder
From the great doors. As those gates fly open, they spin
On their bronze axles fitted by nails and rivets,
Turn in their sockets—one then the other—to make
A wide opening. Straight through them the maidens
Guide the chariot and horses along the broad way.
The Goddess welcomes me warmly, takes my right hand
With her right hand, addresses me and speaks this story:

"O youth, linked with immortal charioteers
And with horses carrying you to our home,
Welcome! It is not at all an evil fate
Sending you forth to come this way, far
From the beaten path of humans, but rather
It is your nature, the order of things,
And your deep urge to listen.

"It is necessary that you hear all things, both
The un-trembling heart of well-rounded truth
And the opinions of mortals, which hold no true belief.

"Nevertheless, you will listen to these also,
How it is necessary that things as they appear
Be acceptable, as they continually penetrate all things."

Eléa's Gate

Clouds today darken the sea to the west.
Wind pulls the sea's smell and distant silence
Up the hillside. We walk the stone road that
Reaches up the hill to the stone gate at the ridge.
Along that way we visit the temple of Asklepios,
Walk inside its walls, invite healing, invite
What we don't yet know we want.

Small green lizards run beside us as we walk.
They move with ease across the ruins, seem
To be without fear, then dart inside small holes
Abundant among still-standing remnants.

At that high ridge the gate opens to the next valley,
Ancestral winds move through it, fervent, wild.
Wedge-shaped stones hold one another in place,
Arc overhead, make the shape of invitation,
Offer passage, night to day, day to night.

December

when the gates of night and day
both open at once,
    and She there waiting;

odd how those gates open,
how decay and ice have not frozen them
    shut,

how the habits of coats and of cobwebs
have not locked them
    into the familiar;

when She speaks spiders tremble
in their webs, Her words pluck
    the strands

of light, of lair, of the long wait for wings
to catch in the mysterious stickiness
    of web;

that inevitable ripening of pears in winter,
their collapse into sugar,
    the music,

how it lifts from plucked string,
escapes from wind blown through narrow wooden
        passage;

again and again Her words, Her story
offering once more
        this thin sip of light

Touched by Stones

I walk where Parmenides walked,
Among the ruins of walls fallen
Since his time, stones that remain
Because they can, because they are
Stones, and in their way speak something
We cannot know, but be touched by
If we listen in stone.

Better maybe to say they *stone,*
Give them the power and standing
Of a verb, one among the many
Chiseled down to a noun, spoken
Over and over, that way we turn
Verbs nouns repeating them until
They fall down, as those walls have fallen,
And now we mostly only remember,
The way a noun might remember
The verb it was when first spoken,
Spoken into being.

I feel the stones awaken,
Begin, how odd, to listen,
Or I imagine it so. Could it
Be they recall through my seeing,

My listening and my imagining
How it was they came to be the walls
That once stood here upright and sturdy,
Each one lifted by gifted hands,
Placed on top of the stone beneath,
Becoming a house, a bath, a temple,
These walls?

I see him clear as day, Parmenides
Walking among the tilted stones,
Offering his right hand in welcome,
And I don't quite know if I imagine it,
Remember it, or if he walks here too
Right *now* beside this water that flows,
Flows from the spring above that gave
This place its name, *Hyéle*.

Three

Parmenides, Fragment II

Come then, I will tell you, and you having heard
The story give heed to it and carry it safely home.

These ways of inquiry alone thinking
Can travel: One that is and is not possible
Not to be, it is a path of Persuasion for it
Accompanies Truth. The other way that is not
And is necessary not to be, I tell you
No news ever comes from that way, for neither
Could you know what is not—for you cannot
Travel there—nor could you utter its sound.

Learning to Speak Fencepost

Were you, Parmenides,
the one who guided me

to stand close
to fenceposts

to listen
to their slivers

their knots
and their uprightness?

Were you there saying
the Goddess is at hand,

that She speaks fencepost,
slivers Her verbs,

knots Her nouns,
the rough touch

of their weathered sides
Her line breaks and rhymes

and that there are almost
no prepositions?

Right There

Wind whistled through the narrow slits between
The fencepost's long splinters, where there was nothing
That I could see, only a flute's sound of nature's making

From the long standing in dry prairie air of any
Wooden post and a farmer's need to have the post
Stand still long enough that, to my young boy sense

Of things, seemed to be forever. It delighted my eyes
And my fingers to touch some thing that lived
Right there inside where forever might arrive,

And there I'd go on many days to touch,
To listen, to see that very nothing and hear
That single forever, and on days when I needed to,

That were many, I'd hold my cheek right there
Where nothing and forever mingled in that way
That wind knew to make audible and to signal,

It seemed maybe only to me, to signal
That if I longed for what was far away
My longing could soothe me, starting at my

Cheek where it touched a body that knew to stand
Still and to wait and to sing, and singing, to weave
Nothing and forever into dancing somewhere

That was nowhere but in that longing.

Parmenides, Fragment III

... for to think and to be are the same.

Winnowing

Wind against the weight of things,
the chaff, the straw, the wheat
makes it all happen.
You don't have to.

What Touched My Shoulder

Parmenides, that road we travel
to the other world,

does it not have the earth beneath
waiting for our feet?

If there were no road to travel
would we find our way?

If no earth below,
would the sun ever set?

Might that yellow evening light
not spread across the hills?

What touched my shoulder
as a boy walking cows to the barn,

would it not speak to me
in its clear voice,

or guide me along the way
to more than this that I took

to be what is, the given,
the unsearched, the uncovered?

Philosopher

Words keep falling from his chest,
tumbling as birds from a nest
who find their wings, feather
the tattered sky.

Parmenides, Fragment IV

Look at things far away as they are, yet
Nevertheless, firmly present to the mind
As they are. For mind does not cut off Being
From things by receiving them, even when
The things are far away, either by dispersing
It all everywhere according to some order,
Or by crowding it together, since the Being
Of things is never far off, nor is it separate
From the things themselves, but always
Everywhere, here, now.

That Sound

Nighthawk cry
Furnace murmur
Wind

Slivered fencepost
My ear so close
A tongue

Loose
A page
A poem

Sunrise
Through that window
Whispers

Arcs over
All day
Sunset

Darkening barn
Hooves clack
Milk-cow

Boot steps

Follow

Stand still

'Til it hums

That song

Beneath

Legs

Pelvic bowl

Remembering

The Way a Stone

There are languages spoken with no verb
"To be." Those who speak them say everything
A people needs to say to grow food to eat
To build a house and sleep; to make love or
Walk alone along a dry creek where stones
Ask for hands to warm them. If you travel
There and don't speak the tongue that says neither
"Is" nor "isn't," stones ask anyway and you know
They want your hands wrapped 'round for just
A little while, then tossed to a new home
Where they wait again, cool their bodies, ready
To be themselves, to speak to anyone passing.

Four

Parmenides, Fragment V

. . . it is one to me from what place I begin,

For to that place I come back again.

Any Day by Shadwell Creek

One step at a time amidst the sun-warmed everything,
my gaze, by chance or not, catches on that place
where my one hand one twig lifts,

riles the dirt dried mud has made, sends tiny tremors
I cannot not imagine to a nearby tree, whose roots so slight
a shift might feel through the shared dirt,

then shiver up her roughened bark, and into each inner ring
that shudders just a bit 'til each high leaf in every vein
receives the unexpected tremor,

unperturbed, I hope, by my intruding touch that reaches
through dirt and nearby tree, and on to each sage bush
and chokecherry limb

until every twig, stone and leaf that lay against
dry Shadwell's bottom, half-way through July,
on not any,

but on this particular day, and not any twig
or stone, but this one only that by seeing
I choose, touch, loosen and lift,

and by that one act maybe change everything for as far as anything
touches what next by it lay, which I imagine never stops
'til China and on beyond all our gravity

and back around to where I stand, not anyplace,
but this place, where, by this one touch it all
begins again to move.

Parmenides, Fragment VI

To speak and to think, Being is, speaking and thinking
Reveal it so, for it is necessary. There is no choice.
Being is and Not-Being is not. That's how it is.
These things I urge you to ponder.

First of all, from this way of inquiry I exclude you,
And afterwards from this other way, on which
Mortals who do not listen wander, two-headed,
For a helplessness in their breasts guides a wandering
Intellect. They are carried along violently,
Dumb and likewise blind, amazed, tribes lacking
Judgment, by whom it has been customarily held
That to be and not to be are the same and not the same,
For whom the path of all things loops back on itself.

Take

Take that thick piece of firewood my dad used
To whip my brother for not putting on the extra
Flannel shirt my mother insisted he wear to walk

In a blizzard the mile and a half to school, turn it
To ash. Take the startled dread I felt at five
Watching this, take my small sliver of empathy,

Glowing hot though it was, turn it to ash too.
Take the alchemist's fire that turns lead to gold.
Take Yeshua's compassion that turns human foibles

Into lessons. Take all of us in that house to a place
Where some day even being wrapped in my mother's
Demons turns to ash or smoke or some particle

Traveling far off where stars wait to take what arrives,
Turn it into some promise, like light maybe.
Or maybe this moment finally finds its black hole,

Gets taken into that singularity beneath
The event horizon where nothing ever happened,
Even this...

Cantilevered

After a blizzard I'd walk the creek looking
For the unexpected little piles of snow
Gathered on a thin limb, resting on old dry
Still-hanging-on leaves, or, best of all,
The wind-driven flakes having tumbled tight
Into each other, their grip steadfast and sure, reaching
Over the creek's ledge to make this perfect curve
Of white snow hanging in mid-air as if, I imagined,
  it were kneeling in quiet prayer.

In this arc of white, a peace so delicious, a stillness
So silent and at rest, to keep it I could not,
For in the keeping there'd be the uncontainable
Urge to touch that would disturb, or the faithless
Looking for a sign of falling, for a blemish in the clean
White edge, or the hint of a dark secret
  under the curved lip of perfection.

When no flaw was to be found, I could not help
But touch and mar the clean edge, bring it too
Into the fallen place I knew, while what I longed
For was just to breathe, kneel down, still as settled
  snow, and never move again.

Parmenides, Fragment VII

For never could this be proved, that Not-Being is.
Exclude thought from this way of inquiry,
And do not let habit born of much experience
Force you to direct an aimless eye and an unquiet
Ear and tongue along this way, but judge
With listening yoked to a clear heart the much
Contested argument which has been spoken by me.

That Want in My Hand

I long for a story as perfect as the stone
I picked up as a kid walking the creek,
The stone, as silent as its voice, as spoken

As its silence. I couldn't help but wonder
If I was hearing something from the stone,
A signal of protest or maybe delight that I'd

Picked it up, chosen it from others nearby.
I wanted to hear what it was the stone might
Be saying in its tongue, its way of breaking

The silence it lived right there where I spotted it
And with that want in my hand, reached for it,
Rubbed loose the dirt that clung to its sides in hopes

I'd hear its faultless tale. While its hard smoothness
Began to warm in the wrap of my palm,
My child mind began its helpless worry

Whether or not I'd disturbed it, maybe
The whole cosmos and me with it just by
Picking it up. All afternoon tromping west

Down the creek I wondered if I should take it back
To where I'd found it. Evening came. I turned
Toward the barn. Late day sunlight began to spread

Its warm and yellow glow around my troubled
Shoulders. That and the stone's slight heft comforted me.
My feet felt the quiet dirt. I grew silent. Without

My knowing how it happened something had settled.
Now, only a boy, a stone in his pocket.

FIVE

PARMENIDES, FRAGMENT VIII

And one utterance of the way still is left, that it is.
Listen to this: On this way are very many signs,
That Being is birthless and indestructible,
For it is whole-limbed and unmoved and without
End; not ever was it or will it be, since
It is now all at once, one, continuous.

For what origin would you seek of Being?
In what way and from where did Being grow?
From Not-Being I shall not allow you to say
Or to think, for it is not to be said or thought
That Being is not.

Beginning from Not-Being, what debt could stir
Being to grow later rather than before?

Hence, it is necessary that Being be either
Wholly or not at all. Not ever will the power
Of trustworthy listening allow that something
Come to be from Not-Being to stand beside Being.

Justice does not loosen the reins enough
On becoming and passing away to allow
Being to either come to be or be destroyed,
But holds them fast: The listening concerning
These things is in this—Being is or it is not.

It has been decided therefore, by Necessity,
That the one way is left unknowable
And nameless, for Not-Being is not a true way.
The other way is and is a true way
For we are listening to it now.

How then could Being be destroyed?
How could it come to be? If it came to be,
It is not, nor if ever it intends to be
In the future. So, coming to be is extinguished,
And destruction of Being we cannot hear
No matter how long we listen.

Neither is Being divisible, since it is all the same,
Neither is there more here or less there which
Could prevent it from holding together, but all
Is completely full of Being. Listening to this
We hear it all, all at once, since all is continuous
With itself, for Being draws near to Being.

Unmoved in limits of great bonds, Being is without
Beginning and without end, since genesis and
Destruction have been made to wander very
Far away; true listening drove them away.

Being remains the same one in the same place
Reposing according to itself, and thus remains
Fixed at the spot, for strong Necessity holds

Being in bonds of a protecting limit which holds
Being back on all sides, because it is not right
That Being be unlimited, for it is not in need;
If it were, it would need everything.

Thinking cannot but mingle with what is thought of,
For not without Being, in regard to which it has
Been spoken, will you find thinking, for nothing
Else either is or will be except Being.
Time past and time future do not exist
Separate from Being, since the Goddess of Fate has
Bound Being with fetters to be whole and unmoved.

Whatever names mortals have laid down without
True listening, having believed them to be true
Will be mere names—to come to be and to be
Destroyed; to be and not to be; to change
Place and to change bright color.

But since there is a last limit, Being is complete
From every side, like the body of a well-rounded
Sphere, equal in the struggle from the middle
In all directions; for it is necessary that there
Be neither something more nor something less
Either here or there. For neither is there Not-Being
Which prevents Being from coming into its like,
Nor is Being more or less than Being,
Since all is safe from violence.

Equal with itself from every side, Being
Hangs together within its own limits.
If you listen, you can hear it.

Here I end my trustworthy account and my
Thought concerning truth; from here on learn
The opinions of mortal men, listening
To the deceitful order of my words.

Mortals posited opinions that named two forms
Of which a unity is not necessary—in this
They are led astray—and they divided these forms
Into contraries and gave them signs separate
From one another. In one place ethereal fire
Of flame, being gentle and very light, the same
To itself in all respects but to that other
Not the same. And black night, that other one,
Also taken by itself and opposite to the other,
Dense in appearance and heavy.

I tell you this whole seeming arrangement so that
No mortal claim for knowing such things
Will ever get past your listening.

Bull Butte

I

Standing still as long as always
It spoke legends from up high.
Always there. North and west
Of our barn. Looking over us.
How I knew I was there.
Not not-there.

Our horse-drawn wagon carried us
West to the little school house across
The creek from the butte. Our teacher,
Jenny Lasinski, at the door.
Bell in hand to summon us. Its sound
Made the butte feel both near and far.

Before and after school, chores waiting.
Worn dirt path carried us to the barn.
Hungry animals watching for us.
Glance west, north. There it was and was
How I knew where I was.

Humble the barn, dark at night,
Home to the unseen ghosts I feared.
Humble the chores. Bucket of oats
To the horses. Dusty, ground grain
To the cow. Fresh milk to feral

Cats. Hay to all the four-leggeds.
Water, always water, to us all.

Back to the house. Bucket of fresh
Milk in one hand made me wobble.
Butte over my right shoulder steadied
Me. It was to my part of earth
What North Star was to my slice of sky.

II

Last summer I return to visit.
Climb to its top. Touch its south-facing,
Sun-warmed sandstone. I remember
Something never quite forgotten,
Never not remembered.

Hands firm against one of its wind-
Shaped, curved shoulders. Feet against
Its ledge. Unexpected vibrations
Enter my arms, move up my legs.
I swear I feel earth's core ablaze
Below. I want that. Not to have it
But to be it, and being it,
To open, to vibrate, become
Molten, not separate and not
Part of everything,
But everything.

Aurora Borealis

At the still point of the turning world. ...
there the dance is, ...
—T. S. Eliot

How is it the fencepost stands so straight
And so alone through the long sunlit day,
Then holds tight and close with sky all night?

How is it this solid standing straight and still
Comes undone when the drunken lights up north
Dance wild over the prairie night sky?

How is it that each post gets gathered
Into that dance, and anyone who stands
Nearby, who dares to touch one of those posts

Is gathered as well into the Northern Light's
Dance? And how is it this one who dares to take
This in, is taken in, breathes and is breathed

Until this one's touch and sight and hearing
Swirl into this wild and crazy choreography,
Its in and out, its up and down, its green

And red, purple and blue? Terpsichore
Turned loose over the prairie.

Six

Parmenides, Fragment IX

So, when all things are named day and night,
And all things according to their powers are
Assigned to one or the other, then all is full
At once of bright day and lightless night,
Of both in equal measure, since nothing
Is left over from either.

Ink and Sin

This morning I sit down with my new fountain pen,
Fill it carefully from the reservoir at the side
Of the bottle, slowly replace the lid and screw
It tight. Then I begin to write across
The empty page—so smooth this indelible
Black ink flows into words, and so smooth my
Memory glides back to when I was little,
And Grandma wrote letters back home to Missoura,
With fountain pens that filled from ink bottles
I loved to touch, to watch the dark body
Of ink sway inside the smooth glass walls with the
Slightest wobble. Each tilt aroused the sly fear
Of a spill I knew would make an indelible mark
Across her desk, her paper, the carpet, someplace
Everyone would see—like sin, as I was taught
By my mother and the Lutherans. Grandma
Wasn't a Lutheran, but she had a face that could
Fire up a fear just like the image of hell
That floated through the church pews Sunday mornings.

I'd sit quiet in church watching my mother's
Face go stone still, hard in the eyes, harder
Than the wooden pew that squeaked with a subtle
Yawn, or a slow turn of the head straining to see
What the men were doing on the benches
At the back, crows gone to sleep along a limb

Where no wind blew, heads tilting at angles of repose,
Shirt pockets bulging with packs of cigarettes
I knew they'd light up as soon as they walked
Outside at the end of all the talk from the pulpit
About fire and sin and the savior's hands receiving
The awful nails for us, always for us.

At my Grandma's desk I'd weigh the odds, take
A careful twist to test how tight the lid
Was closed, then tilt the bottle slightly to watch
The black body of ink climb one side then
The other, leaving, for moments, a thin veil
Of itself clinging to the inside walls of the
Darkened glass. Wasn't it trying to leave
This glassy prison, waiting to be drawn into
The small barrel of the green or the red pen,
Waiting to become a letter of the alphabet,
A word in one of Grandma's sentences,
Then to dry and lie still across the crisp
White paper from her thick tablet and be folded
Inside an envelope with a three cent stamp?
She'd send me off to the post office, across
The street at the end of her block, then across
The other street to the red brick building with
"U.S. POST OFFICE"
Etched in the stone lintel over the door.

Once inside, another world shown off the murals
Of Frederick Remington, off the shiny marble
Floor, and off the walls where "WANTED" posters
Showed tough faces of people I knew had sinned,
Spilled blood maybe, like ink, across someone's shirt,
And now their faces were on the wall for all
To see. I'd shiver at the thought that my face
Could appear there, hold my breath as I slid past
The bulletin board and over to the mail slot,
Where I'd read three times to make sure it was
The one Grandma had shown me, where letters
Were supposed to go. Finally I'd let it fall
From my hand, wondering if I'd done it right.
When I was sure I'd done nothing wrong, my mind
Would fly off into its wondering about that ink,
Now gone still on Grandma's letter, with its job
Of saying something to someone far off in Missoura,
Who I'd never met, but knew was waiting to hear
How we were doin'. I longed for a job so clear,
So clean, so done now that no sin could happen
By mistake by my hand, or my mind, which still moved,
Like the ink in the bottle, and anything was waiting
To happen in this world where a sin could put
Your face on one of those posters, forever.

Parmenides, Fragment X

From a high enough place and with an open eye
And ear you will learn the nature of the heavens
And all its signs that shine, as well as the hidden
Works of the undefiled sun's pure torch,
And from whence they all came.

You will also learn the deeds and the nature
Of the wandering round-eyed moon.

Then you will come to know embracing-everything
Heaven, know whence it was born, and how Necessity
Came up with a way to fetter the stars within limits.

An Unexpected Quiet

I watch dust motes float in the hayloft when
Afternoon light slants against our barn's west

Side and streams through cracks between its shrinking
Weathered boards. If I keep my gaze on one

Of those streams of sunlight, sooner or later
A single particle of dust moves as if

Weightless through that stream, ignites
For a moment into an orb of light

That fills the entire loft, me inside it,
With an unexpected quiet, its touch

As delicate as oats in the nearby bucket.

Parmenides, Fragment XI

...how earth and sun and moon and the shared heaven
Along with the heavenly milk and outermost Olympos
And the warm life-blood of the stars all passionately
Set themselves in motion to come into being...

Heavenly Milk

After the cow births her calf
My dad lights a smoke. We move to a hill
Far enough back not to bother them,

Getting to know each other the first
Time in light of day. He rests on his
Haunches, lights another and watches,

A smile curves his mouth, blue smoke curls
Into still air. We wait while the calf
Finds its feet, stumbles to the cow's udder,

Drinks its first milk. Two cigarettes
Later, I know I want to smoke
When I grow up. Sounds of frothy

Sucking drift like a hymn across
The silence we share with calf, cow,
Melting snow and gods, all of them

Waiting to be fed. The thin blue
Smoke keeps dancing, remains of snow
Give way, a crocus here another there

Punctuate mud and tender grass.
It isn't church, but better.

Parmenides, Fragment XII

For the narrower bands are filled with pure fire
And the next ones with night, and in the midst
Of these a portion of flame is sent forth.

In the middle of this the Goddess steers all things.

For everywhere she begins sexual mingling
And the painful drama of birthing, sending
The female to mix with male and again the
Other way around, the male with the female.

It Goes On

This time I'm fourteen and he says, *It's your turn.*

When the next contraction hits, her body groans,
a sound someplace between pain and pleasure
passes between my own ribs.

          One foot appears, not two;
naked to the shoulder, between contractions
I reach in, blind hand finds what I've already seen,
          only one front hoof.

I reach deeper, fingers swimming upstream,
          as if entering a dream,
the cow seems miraculously not bothered
          by my presence inside her.

Then it comes, next wave of her push,
she grips my arm with her birth canal,
          nothing more sure of itself.
All four of her legs stiffen,
          and as her moan cleaves the air,
I'm suddenly stilled inside her.

Only minutes ago she tried to run us down.
Now I've become part of her,
          smell of winter's straw, manure,

dirt and wet cow's tail—all of it so close to my face
            there is no room to doubt this world.

An unexpected peace enters my body.

Inside her dark, the other leg touches my farthest
finger, which cannot move until her contraction ends.

The moment she relaxes, I reach deeper,
grab the folded knee and with my feet
braced against the ground,
            push the small body back
                        where there's more room,

all the way to where I find the backward foot,
grip its slippery hoof,
flip it forward to join the other,
lace my fingers around the leg bones,
tighten my grip and wait.

            When it comes, I pull, pull with her push,
my arm as intimate with her as strange to itself,
little one sliding into sight, two front feet,
            legs, pink nose, white face, ears slicked back,
                        long red body,

all of it sliding onto the exhausted straw.

DEEP DISTURBANCE

Making a calf born bull into a steer
was common practice on the ranch,
but the first time it fell to me to perform
the act it was anything but common.

My entire body wrenched against itself
with each single and clumsy move I made.
The knife, sharpened to its surgical
edge, slid dangerously between my fingers.

When the castration was finished,
I felt its deep disturbance, as if something
had happened there, in my own groin;
something between pressure and hollowed

out, a sensation I've never forgotten,
one of those body memories psychotherapists
search for in trauma work when naming
how the body hangs onto its history without

words, stored in the tissue, its cells tied together
in knots, and when this one awakens, unties itself,
I hear the calf's helpless cry.

Seven

Parmenides, Fragment XIII

She devised Eros as the very first of all the gods...

Juneberry Picking

Our mothers, excited when a good crop
Of Juneberries ripen, rare on the prairie,
Take us, the neighbor girl and me, along.

Worried by the unexpected rattlesnakes
In the grass, they leave us in the car where we
Watch them descend into the creek to pick

The gorgeous purple fruit. We wait, we play,
We see light rise from our small flesh, mine
And hers, take delight with the taut skin of our

Legs tingling toe to crotch. A garden we did
Not know beckons. We enter. Our eyes and hands
Harvest delicious, innocent fruit. She wants

To see how mine works. I pee off the running
Board, careful to stay in the car as we were told,
Arc my yellow stream into the forbidden grass

Where snakes might wait. As she watches she touches.
We abandon ourselves to drunken delight until
Two bodies, heads first, rise from the creek. My

Mother's eyes fill with horror at sight of my
Beautiful arc. A dark cloud fills the open sky.
Something sharp, like I imagine a snake's bite,

Enters my body, stuns the wild tingling still.

Parmenides, Fragment XIV

Wandering around the earth shining in the night

With a borrowed light.

Him on His White Horse, Me on My Pinto

It was quiet across the hills of our summer pasture
When, horseback with my father, we'd check the cows
With their calves to make sure none were sick or ailing,
Or had escaped the fence into another's pasture.

We'd count them as we rode, a kind of praying
Or offering of liturgy. If the count came out right
There was peace, and the very earth, with its hills
And its grasses, seemed almost to smile at the sky,
And in that between of earth and sky, we rode
Our horses, gentle like the breeze that visited
The tall grass stems, making them bow down
In what felt like a gesture of gratitude that we
Were gathered into as we rode along,
Counting one by one.

On our approach to each gathering of cows, ten
To fifteen or fewer, each of them, head down, grazing,
Their calves nearby sleeping, nestled into swirls of grass
They'd made by lying down as they turned, the way
Our dog lay down, circling his body into repose.

My father had taught me by his example and by
His word to approach each sleeping calf slowly

And at the right distance to not startle the sleeping
One awake into a run, but to watch as each stood up
Slow enough to take its time to stretch that way
Mammals, when they feel well, do on rising.

If a calf failed to stretch it signaled something
Might be wrong and we'd watch it pair up
With its mother. If her udder was swollen
We'd tend to the calf as was needed.

If she was empty we'd know the little one
Was nursing, that things were okay, and we'd
Move on, the answer given.

Spike

I

I love that stumblebum pinto, love him like a brother,
a lover. Though he stumbles too much to trust,
I want to trust someone so much I ride him

even after he somersaults me under him, perfectly
upside-down, both of us startled and dizzied.
Rising, grateful to be in one piece, I pat his neck

which trembles like my hand, lift myself into the saddle,
and we go on.

II

Spike's breath on my cheek at the top of a hill,
soft, like the touch of dust on a cow path.

His nose as smooth as the silk around my pillow case
that I gather into my small hand at night.

III

When we chase the yearling colts, my dad and me silent,
me knowing he wants me different, wants me to ride faster,
not hold back when they get close to the gate, not let them

slip away again to race back to the far corner of our pasture,
a mile the other way. The next time they race ahead of us,
a half mile to the gate and crowding my side, I urge Spike along,

but still caught inside my mother's fear, not yet in my father's
abandon, I hold back on the reins, eyes scanning for hoof-size
prairie dog holes, watching Spike's feet fly over the ground.

At some moment I have not planned, someplace inside me
that thread back to the house and to her fear snaps.
I let the reins go loose, nudge Spike hard with my spurs...

Inside my virgin head I hear these words,
fuck it, let's go, I could die,
and the lust inside abandon takes me, sound of hoof beats

like thunder, Spike and me crowding up against them,
driving them through the gate,
my dad and me yipping as we gallop.

Parmenides, Fragment XV

Always keeping an eye out for the light of the sun.

It's Winter

It's thirty-five below zero.
Our prairie shack's walls barely
Stop the cold even while the coal
Furnace blazes its fervent murmur
Through the living room where its fire
Glows inside its cast iron cage
All night long.

Our white enamel wash basin, chipped
Black edge, holding leftover water
From someone's late night hand washing,
Stands on its small wooden table
At the kitchen's far end, too far
For the furnace's warmth to reach.

Morning comes. My mother turns it
Upside down. No water falls. Seems
Like a trick to me, that way it holds
Water with dirt from someone's hands
And evening chores.

Makes me think of the trapeze artist
In the circus that came to our town,
How he hung upside down, held
Another's body from falling.

My dad starts the kitchen's cook
Stove fire. Its heat takes a while
To reach where the wash basin stands
Still and heavy with its burden of ice.

Its water finally melts. She pours
It into the slop bucket that stands
Beside the little table. It makes
That sound we all were waiting for
Of something frozen coming loose.

Getting to Zero

There are grander stories than this one,
But what I remember well, waiting by my
Father's side, was watching while the banker

Wrote the sums, multiplied by the interest,
Divided by the heifers, and spoke in his dry
Locust voice, pack of Lucky Strikes sitting

Crooked on his wide wooden desk—*Well, this*
Is how I think we'll work it—But I knew
The only one who'd work would be my father,

And the only consolation would be knowing
His work was in the dirt, worth sweating for,
Made him smile from the edge of the field

When he looked out over the young green shoots
Of wheat making their way to August, ripening
Into bone white, when the softest breeze sets

The dry heads to singing, to singing their
Shimmering harvest song, ripening into his
Bones that I carry in some uncovered grave,

Waiting for the banker to get to zero.

EIGHT

Parmenides, Fragment XVI

As the mixture of much-wandering limbs goes,
So thought comes to humans. For as each human
Wanders, always seeking balance, the mind
Sets forth its guidance. It is the same for all,
The mind guiding the wandering limbs.
Whatever mind does beyond this is thinking.

Someplace

Just as little is seen in pure light
as in pure darkness.
—Georg Wilhelm Friedrich Hegel

Wind chimes next door
Listen, they sound free
Someplace a horse is running right now

Someplace a polar bear is resting on ice
Wind moves across the curve of earth like a glove
Listen, grass says, it is here

Any place, opposites move toward the next imperfection
Wind, for example
Listen, you can hear leaves tremble

Someplace a grasshopper nibbles on the tender wheat
Stops to spit, chews, leaps to the next stalk
A child sees this, mimics it with his whole body

Listen, someplace we sing the last song
The place they pull us free from breathing this air

The Day I Stopped Hunting Deer

The doe stepped innocent as air
from the creek into the field,
her large ears scanning.

October's prairie sun
setting behind her,
its light turning everything yellow.

Head down,
she grazed in the tall grass,
looked up, then down again to graze.

Still as settled dust,
I sat in my truck,
raised my rifle.

Her ears flickered back and forth,
light glistened over her whole body.
When my finger wrapped 'round the trigger,

that light touched the gun-metal gray.
I adjusted the aim,
waited,

did not shoot,
drove away...

PARMENIDES, FRAGMENT XVII

On the right, male; on the left, female.

Remembering the First Time I See an Elephant

Nothing like them had ever visited our town, unless we count Wooly
Mammoths who roamed there one-hundred-thirty-thousand years ago.
I once saw a picture and noticed they had smaller ears than elephants.
This morning I walk down Madison Street in Asheville, North Carolina.
Huge leaves of a nearby Colocasia plant stir something in me.

An elder woman working in the front yard tells me they're called
Elephant Ears. At that moment I'm back in Sidney, Montana, nineteen-
fifty-four. Barnum and Bailey brought three elephants all the way
to our little prairie town. Inside the circus tent I sit next to my father
and watch the tug of war, one elephant and a big green tractor,
arranged by the John Deere dealer to show off his equipment.

My mother is in Denver, Colorado, at a mental hospital. Her letters
arrive infrequently, words of missing us between notes of outings
they've taken her on that she's liked. They make her feel farther
away than the sound of the word, *Denver.*

The gracious elephant stands still and quiet. Looking at her huge ear,
I feel happy for no reason I know. Someone shoots a gun to signal
the beginning of the contest. The tractor revs up, sends out its smoke
and noise. The elephant handler signals her to start pulling. She leans

into her harness. Only a few moments in I swear I see the handler
with his long stick, sharp hook at the end, grab the elephant by her ear,
nudge her to step backward when it's clear as day to me she's winning.

I wonder why that man makes her stop pulling, and I want to ask my
father, who sits so close I could touch him and whose skin, weathered
in wind, surprises me how much it looks like the elephant's hide,
but I don't ask for fear I'll burst into tears.

Two Infinities

High on his wire,
the tight rope walker
looks down,
waits for his nerves
to settle
and tries his weight.

The crowd's hushed silence
enters his legs.

Nourished, he steps
onto air divided
into two infinities.

The soles of his feet
defeat fear again
as his urge to fly
leans on the wings
of a thousand eyes.

Nine

Parmenides, Fragment XIX

So, according to belief, these things were brought
Forth and now are, and afterwards, from this time,
They will grow and perish. And for each of these things,
Humans have laid down a distinguishing name.

Note to Parmenides

One day the sun was shining
and I rode my father's white horse

across the wide summer pasture.
It must be that maidens of the sun guided me

for when I rode to the round wooden water tank
just before the mare's muzzle rippled the surface

I felt the perfection of still water
settle into my belly

and for a moment
nothing moved.

Then I listened as each swallow
passed down her long gullet.

When the water stilled again
we turned to leave.

My Father's Visit

He arrived so unexpectedly, stood
So lifelessly still in the middle of my
Little grad school apartment at Penn State,

Further east than he'd ever traveled.
Three years since his heart stopped on top of the little
Hill in Montana, riding Babe, his best horse ever,

To find and doctor a sick cow. Stripped of his
Pitchfork, his milk bucket, his camel cigarette,
Even his legs seemed missing, only that slight,

Crooked smile and familiar cock of his head.
Beethoven's late string Quartet, slow movement,
Op. 132, A minor, ascending from where the needle

Traveled along its black groove in the record
From where Ludwig sang, as if he too were visiting.
In the dim light, middle of night, after the grad

Student party while sitting alone, listening intently,
The stillness of nobody there with me interrupted
By his presence. Nearly silent, the sound of his arrival,

Him watching, but not watching, seeing me
As I'd never been seen by him. His chest draped
In the common blue work shirt, but no body

Inside it, his face a shadowy likeness,
And so quiet without the ever-present worry
For crops and cows. My unwept grief spilled

As I listened to Beethoven's Molto
Adagio, written after he too
Had come near to dying.

The Open and Close of It

In the Egyptian section of the New York
Metropolitan Museum of Art, I walk past two
Wooden statues in an enclosed glass space dated
2350 BCE. The one on the left, a householder figure
I imagine, stands straight and simple, a wooden staff
In each hand, simple headdress, a belted skirt
Hangs from his hips to his knees. All down its front
A deep crack in the wood exposes its darker, inner grain.

On my first pass I try to ignore the crack
And see the statue. On my second time walking by,
The crack captures me. How long, I wonder,
Has it been there? How did it look before?
I can't push away the feeling that the statue
Asks me to listen to its fissure, how it speaks
For the statue, for the imperfect, for all coming apart,
For how coming apart might be what bodies do,
They break open and show what's underneath.

This crack speaks for what is unspoken, for what's
Sturdy enough to dare to fall apart, for what
Has been whole and now isn't, though still standing
And fierce, open to something not yet known.

Does it not speak for what is old and broken,
And too, for what is young, for when this figure

Was conceived, for what wants to stay young and can't?
Maybe it speaks, as well, for the large elm trees
Along the creek, the sycamores along Memorial Drive,
For the standing pine that will be taken for lumber, cut
By axes and saws into boards that remember the tree.

Not less than all of this, the crack, and all I can imagine
Of it, all I can love, enacting love that ages, that breaks,
That opens, wants to close to save itself and can't.
It voices what we want yet can't name. It's that sculptor's
Longing for something, the carved man's longing, everyone's
Longing who walks past this statue, and me with them.

I'm in that crack. I'm wanting that crack to close, to open,
To heal, to fall apart, wanting it to take me back
To where I come from. I want the open and close of it,
The standing tall, the refusal to go away,
The want to declare—this is what is.

The name for what, alone, is fully untroubled is *to be.*

PARMENIDES, FRAGMENT XX

ACKNOWLEDGMENTS

Thanks to Homebound Publications where a few of the poems in this book, though in different versions, appeared in an earlier book of mine, *Having Listened,* (Homebound Publications, 2013). Those poems include "Horses Could Take You There," "Winnowing," "Philosopher," "Cantilevered," (titled "After a Blizzard"), "Ink and Sin," "Someplace," "Note to Parmenides."

And thanks to the poetry journal, *Salamander,* for having published "Parmenides, Fragment I," (titled "Listen," and in a slightly different version), *Salamander* #48, ed. by Fred Marchant, guest editor, and Jennifer Barber, founding editor, Summer 2019.

Locus Amoenus (then untitled) was originally published in an essay of mine titled, "Henry Bugbee as Mentor," which appeared in a collection of essays in his honor titled, *Wilderness and the Heart: Henry Bugbee's Philosophy of Place, Presence, and Memory,* (The University of Georgia Press, ed. By Edward F. Mooney, 1999).

"It Goes On," in a slightly different version, originally appeared in *Narrative* magazine, 2017.

I would also like to express my deep gratitude to all who have helped and supported me along the way of creating this book:

To all those at the Brookline Poetry Series whose listening to earlier versions of many of these poems has given the priceless support that comes from participating in the oral tradition of poetry.

To wonderful friends from both near and far, Sally Moore, Roger Dunsmore, Jeff Stark, Sasha Badkhen, Marina Badkhen, Mark Pevzner, David Elliott, Halvor Kjølstad, Dagrun Dvergsdall, Lisa Lancaster, Deb Dana, Andrew James Brown, Ed Mooney, Lisa Mowery, Charlie Munitz and Yaron Carmel, whose voices of encouragement have been a steady presence along the way.

To my family members, Elizabeth, Anna, Soren, Jeremy, Liam, Ella and Addi, who have witnessed my writing endeavor and encouraged me in their different ways over many years.

To dear friends, Anna Badkhen, Rich Borofsky, Martha Collins, Kim Garcia, Frank Garcia, Aimée Sands, the late Alan Albert, Susan Nissenbaum Becker, Jennifer Barber and Fred Marchant, who have given generous support to this project, and have offered specific and thoughtful suggestions for numerous poems in this collection.

To my partner, Sabine Boots, whose steady ear and intuitive listening to multiple versions of many of these poems has helped the poems and has sustained and nourished me in times of doubt.

To my good friends, David Ferry and George Kalogeris, my deepest heartfelt thanks for their unwavering support, their generous listening to and reading of this entire manuscript, offering many helpful suggestions along the way, and whose poems and translations of ancient texts have been abiding inspiration and guidance to me as I have continued to find my voice and my way while bringing this collection of poems and this translation of Parmenides' fragments into being.

And finally, I am deeply grateful to the staff at Homebound Publications, in particular to Connor Wolfe, whose confidence in this project, their offer to publish this collection, their artistry and skill in making books, and their gracious shepherding of the process have made this book possible.

NOTES

"*Locus Amoenus*": the epigraph is quoted from *The Inward Morning: A Philosophical Exploration in Journal Form,* by Henry Bugbee, (The University of Georgia Press, 1999). p. 163.

On Translating Parmenides:

As a grad student in philosophy, translating Parmenides' poem from the classical Greek opened a floodgate of remembering my life on the prairie. That remembered prairie life became a vehicle for traveling into the language of Parmenides' poem, finding there a voice that both touched me and brought something I was already carrying into the light for me. Remembered fenceposts and my standing next to them, exploring their weathered sides and imagining what they had seen and heard standing there at one spot all that time became metaphors that pointed toward the stillness I began to glimpse in the well-placed words of Parmenides.

I'd sit for a long time next to a phrase of the Greek, waiting to hear it in its own terms, hoping to move nearer to Parmenides' sense of Being as expressed through his well-crafted hexameter lines that so beautifully and elegantly do what they say. I now see that Parmenides was with me all the way. His spirit guided me on the prairie, helped me open before I knew I was opening or that there was help.

Someplace along the way of this translating journey, I began to imagine that standing next to a Greek phrase, waiting to catch its idiosyncratic lean toward its potential meanings was not so different from standing next to those fenceposts as a kid, feeling drawn toward their stillness, their ever-presence, signaled in the sound of wind fluttering through the splinters on the weathered side of an old pine or cedar post. The solidity of weathered wood against the movement of wind, the earth below me feeling still even while spinning, all of it conveyed into my body an interweaving of movement and stillness toward which Parmenides' poem pointed in word and sound as I came to hear it. It was in this standing next to Parmenides' Greek phrases that I began to remember the longing I felt while standing next to the fenceposts, the longing for "what stands still a long time."*

In my effort to translate Parmenides' poem I came to realize in retrospect that I was being initiated into a practice of listening. My struggle with the ancient text of his poem, its vocabulary, grammar and syntax, was the beginning of a journey. Parmenides was exhorting me, his reader, to enter fully into this engagement of listening, not only to his text and what it reveals by enacting it, but also to my own journey of recollecting where I'd come from. It's what his poem asks of anyone who chooses to take up with it. The opening of that granary full of memories from my childhood became part of the listening journey, calling me to re-member, to uncover, to recognize hard truths as well as to appreciate what had been offered in that young life on the prairie. This journey has become for me a process of restoration, taking me back to myself in the deepest sense.

Thank you for listening to Parmenides with me through my rendering of the fragments we have of his poem. I choose to call what I offer here "a version from the Classical Greek" rather than a translation. Starting from the literal translation I did in my twenties, and over the years consulting my trusty ancient Greek dictionary, along with numerous translations that others have done, I have attempted to offer a version of the poem that rings true to Parmenides' fifth century BCE text and to his poetic voice as we are able to hear it in our twenty-first century listening.

*"what stands still a long time"
from "To Fencepost"
a poem in my earlier book, *Having Listened*

"*Eléa's* Gate": *Eléa* is the name of the place where Parmenides lived in the 5th century BCE, on the southwestern coast of Italy, about 25 miles south of the famous cite of many ruins, *Paestum*. The name *Eléa* was changed to *Velia* in the Roman era.

—Asklepios is the ancient Greek God of healing and medicine.

"Touched by Stones": *Hyéle* is the name of the spring and stream that flows from the ridge around the parameter of the city, *Eléa*, whose name derives from *Hyéle*.

"Aurora Borealis": Terpsichore is the name for the ancient muse of dance.

—the epigraph to this poem is quoted from *Four Quartets, Burnt Norton*, by T. S. Eliot, (Harcourt Brace Jovanovich, 1943). P. 15.

"Someplace": the epigraph is quoted from *The Science of Logic*, by Georg Wilhelm Friedrich Hegel, translated by George Di Giovanni, (Cambridge University Press, 2010). P. 77.

"My Father's Visit": Beethoven apparently wrote the Molto Adagio movement to his String Quartet No. 15 in A minor, Op. 132, in 1825, after recovering from a serious illness which he had feared would be fatal.

About the Author

Grandson of homesteaders, Gary Whited grew up on a cattle ranch in eastern Montana in the 1940's and 50's. When he left the ranch to study philosophy, he had no idea he was about to encounter ancient Greek thinkers who would take him back to the ranch. The kinship he felt between the thought of early Pre-Socratic philosophers and the sense of a profound interconnectedness of all things that he'd experienced growing up on the prairie intrigued him. His doctoral dissertation explored that kinship and resulted in his first translation of the fragments of Parmenides' fifth century BCE poem.

Being, There offers his current version of that translation project along with some of his new poems. Whited's rendering of this ancient text together with his poems respond to the call from Parmenides to listen to what claims us and speaks to us, and through that deep listening to uncover the presence of Being in each encounter, each moment.

After teaching philosophy for several years at University of Montana, University of Texas and Emerson College in Boston, Gary began to study and practice psychotherapy. Over the years it has become clear to him that the listening that began in the silent presence of fenceposts and the subtleties of the prairie landscape has carried him to the ancient Greek classical voices, to his students in philosophy classes and eventually to his clients in psychotherapy sessions.

Whited has published several essays in journals and anthologies in the fields of philosophy and psychology. He has also lectured and facilitated workshops internationally on the healing of unresolved grief, shame, and trauma.

His first book of poems titled, *Having Listened,* won the 2013 Homebound Publications Poetry Contest. In 2014 it received a Benjamin Franklin Silver Book Award. *Having Listened* was translated into Russian and made into a bilingual volume also published by Homebound Publications.

His poems have appeared in journals, including *Salamander, Plainsongs, The Aurorean, Atlanta Review, Narrative, The Red Letters* and *Comstock Review.*

Gary currently lives in Cambridge, Massachusetts.

WAYFARER